Praise for *All Things Can Be True*

With beautifully layered personal insight and universal beliefs, Deyanira illustrates the complexities of self-discovery, resilience, & cultural identity. An honest and astonishing poetry collection encouraging a more compassionate and empathetic understanding of ourselves & each other.

—Crystal Reyes, author of *Wildflower Blooming*

All Things Can Be True is a tastefully tender yet emboldened invitation to untangle our sense of self in the worlds we reside in. Contreras' debut collection is nothing less than the security of a hand to hold, a companion of words sewn together with intentionality, and a mezcla of poetry crafted to walk you home. I have yet to come across a collection that is more of a mirror than *All Things Can Be True*. This quilt of poems calls to action my own reflection asking it to set itself free. In these pages of liberation, are a craving, comfort and finding of self acceptance, a liberating display of our taboos, and a welcoming embrace of the kaleidoscopes found in our identities. Contreras is an author-architect-artist of a universal roadmap to carry with us, as we paint the canvas of our truths, daringly, openly, and with full audacity.

—RAVINA, author of *Yellow*

Through her insightful gaze, Contreras invites us into a world of profound human connection and raw vulnerability, revealing the beauty and courage in sharing our most intimate selves.

—Andrés Sánchez, author of *This Body*

ALL THINGS CAN BE TRUE

ALL THINGS CAN BE TRUE

Deyanira Contreras

All Things Can Be True / Todo Puede Ser Cierto
© 2025 Deyanira Contreras
ISBN: 979-8-9893829-9-6

Published by Mama's Kitchen Press
Austin, TX / Los Angeles, CA
www.mamaskitchenpress.com

First Trade Paperback Original Edition, 2025

Manufactured in the United States of America

Cover Art & Design by Kimberly Gaeta Brown
Layout Design by Emily Anne Evans

This is dedicated to you. Perhaps we've never met and never will. Even so, may you see yourself with grace and compassion. May you feel a bit more human while reading these truths—which are only mine as I've discovered them—thoughts that have saved me from myself at times, words I aim to incorporate into daily endeavors and find in my way of being.

Take from it what you need.
Thank you for finding this (or for it finding you.)

Table of Contents

Preface

All Things Can Be True is a collection of what I have come to understand throughout my life up to this point.

It is a combination of wit, sarcasm, desire, bravery, and pleasure. It is a journey to understand myself and my place in the world.

I have realized that I am, as we all are, in constant evolution and transformation—that we are more alike than we are different.

I want my writing to be reflective of the vulnerability we possess as human beings in an effort to be kinder, softer, and more empathetic toward each other.

We are all just trying to live—to do our best—and whether we understand it or not, we're not getting out alive!

So, may our encounters be plenty, our dance eternal, and may we make our own dreams come true each day.

ALL THINGS CAN BE TRUE

The right to write

I own the boldness required
to survive a seemingly unscathed childhood,
to exhale the ghosts of innocence preyed on by ignorance and love.
To resume a treacherous adolescence
exceeding the normalcy of raging hormones,
transcending all expectations of lessons learned.

Each written word a design
in the protective armor of self-advocacy,
an appealing defense of all endured up to this point.

In each phrase, a self-fulfilling prophecy,
all about me since I am what I know.
I am a lifelong research.
Myself at every moment, though often unbeknown.

I've come to terms with its narcissistic tendencies.
Personal and protected.
Each line break a mirror image
of heart-rending emotions that consumed me at the time.
Each word insignificant until set ablaze by the burst of a memory.

I write to pretend I understand how to live,
to make sure there is some documentation
of the insecurities and triumphs,
at times full force and afraid; others, fragile and desperate.
In each phrase, the possibility of a heightened perspective.

It takes time to find the precise words.
There's no technique, and the grammar is most likely off.
But it does have the rhythm of every heartbeat and pulse.
An instinctive and escalating climax of emotion and vitality
in words that bring rest and regulation to an aching soul.

Say my name

Despite your discomfort
and its taste in your mouth,
Say my name.
Flavor the chalky residue
of premise and assumption
upon a botched pronunciation.
Savor the forthcoming dread
of incapability,
swallow your spit,
clear your throat,
Say my name.
In syllables if you must–,
four to provide clarity,
sound out the consonants,
enunciate the vowels that follow,
flex your tongue,
articulate and evolve
past your cultural incompetency.

Say my name,
take a breath,
pause when necessary,
try again.
Rest assured
after the first time
you'll remember.
It is abstract.
and requires a certain effort,
but it's more relatable
than you'd think;
complex and intense
enough to leave you yearning
for an opportunity
to say it again and again,
each time in revindication,
Say my name,
feel it slide like honey
down your throat,
let it coat your insecurities
and be merciful upon
your judgment.

Existential stroll

Every step taken outside my body,
      a faint imprint to mark the way back,
      like breadcrumbs on a trail,
      or what's left of them upon my arrival.

Pieces of me scattered upon drenched soil,
      emotions once cupped gently in trembling hands
      spilled onto an undiscovered path, water seeds frozen in time;
      stillness set in motion by a whistling wind
      and an onset of silence.

I head back to me, a much celebrated arrival.
      Atemporality suspended in that vague space
      where neither foot is touching the ground,
      just before a legacy indents on wet soil.

Wherever I find myself,
      I head back home
walking with reclaimed perspective,
      a firm step,
      on sore feet and solid legs.

I'm reminded to breathe.
      Inhale methodically
      to a count of four,
to keep present and forging forward.
      Exhale profoundly to a count of eight
to lead me home.

      Walking back
      on an unmarked trail,
      on sore feet and solid legs,
      on instinct, impulse, and fluttering joy.

You: an inverted perspective

She walks anticipating the next explosion,
       weighed down by residual memories,
       caught on the soles of her shoes.
A body suspended in the agony of purgatory,
       condemned to the absence of comfort.

Mind racing past secluded memories,
       with miniscule care on limber steps
       so as to not disturb the battlefields.
Lingering mechanisms of survival.
eyes wide open to the one
yellow daffodil protruding from barren ground.

Tears slither down her face despite clenched lids,
       subdued by this tiny miracle,
       her being its only recipient.
Thoughts perturbed by unanswered questions,
       that have paved repeated doubt and
       unsettling responses revealed
       in vibrant imagery against the will of time.

And though stillness does not become her,
       escape is no longer an option.
Shaken and disturbed by the strange comfort of life's battles,
she fights the constant temptation to disappear among the multitudes,
       to evaporate in a last breath,
       to chase one last high.
But healing requires presence.

She walks shield in hand,
       protected by instinct,
       fighting on impulse–necessary or not.
Her heartbeat is the only reminder of transparency.
       When she withdraws from joy, I taste her tears and shiver at her agony.
       When she delights in sunlight, her laughter lights my soul.

Catalyst

She who searches a space on earth
to come back to when encounters prove fickle,
confirming we're all on the same journey.

She who inhabits a body of evidence,
bearing witness to the insignificance of living,
to rage otherwise silent if ignored,
to the echo that lingers long after her absence.

She who attracts intensity and longs for its
resurrective tendencies, allowing for a
brief frolic in nostalgia and reminiscence,
of glimmering memories and rumbling bones,
until the abrupt awareness at the lack of resistance.

She who adjusts,
categorizes,
alphabetizes,
placing every injustice in order of severity,
acquitting multiple perpetrators on the basis of good intentions.

She who repels misery but also longs for its company,
a peaceful coexistence.
Maintaining the soul fragile enough to keep her honest.

Catalyst.
By definition: she who provokes chaos in search of peace
because, logically, one does not exist without the absence or presence of the
other.

By default: a fully admissible premise to a post-traumatic existence
in a body that's also the recipient of the love and pleasure it's been shown.

She who gathers herself piece by piece.
In every caress, an opportunity to reframe.
In every scar, a battle wound transformed.

I never signed a DNR

I've made love to three women on that bed.

When it was first purchased,
I knew I wanted it to be
strong enough to withstand times of turbulence,
to withhold the transformation from communal slumbers,
        to partnership, to marriage.

Solid wood to hold regenerative sleep -
peaceful, restless, anxious
or temporary insomnia.

I'd never thought about any of those requirements
        until I considered getting rid of it.
Once grandiose and seemingly perfect,
now bulky and excessive.

Three phases.
Three stages.
Three women.
A variety of weight, hair lengths, personalities,
and a once-marked road between desolation and despair.

Solid wood to hold darkness,
frustration,
        desire,
        complacency,
        tenderness,
        some pleasure,
        tears, and

Silence.

I've made love to three women on that bed,
and through it all,
only one indentation remains on the right side of the headboard.

Three women have laid, and one has arisen.

Female

The divine feminine
is carried somewhere in the soul.
Regardless of genitals,
biology, or assignment at birth.
  Exquisite.
  Delightful.
Mouthwatering curves,
eyes and lashes,
breasts and thighs for days,
  lower back indentations
that bring sheer and utter pleasure;
a parallel longing.

A beauty that I now feel inside.
A plain and simple love
for this body that has carried me,
through indignation & shame,
through thoughts of self-annihilation–
neither prudent nor ingenious.
A cruel punishment for my loyalty to life.

According to society's standards,
I should have looked a certain way and never have.
I should have done certain things and never did.
Futile attempts prevented me from exploring a perspective
I knew was there
since I was 2 feet shorter and not as wide,
before a lingering adolescence took its last breaths,
I looked at life and felt it in silence,
accumulating secrets
mysteries to be deciphered at a later time,
held in a body that kept enlarging past its limits,
inhabiting and cohabiting its demise and glory.

The crow: a generational curse

You were gone long before I arrived.
Even so, your silent presence remained,
in the few seconds of silence before each infant let out the first cry.
A mandate of secrecy granted throughout the lineage of those
born from your descent.

Legend says,
you called full house to a pair of aces and a third of nines.
Clammy hands held death grip and destiny
in a precise combination of luck and wit.
All or nothing was the game;
and nothing it was.
The hand and your soul, face down,
you handed over your life and,
with it, resignation and complacency as genetic traits.

I felt you in my father's silence and long exhales,
both so dense and lacking any element of surprise,
as if life had already dealt him its worst hand.

You hover as a foggy existence
dark skin and obsidian eyes,
diluted through every generation that followed.
Excluding your sons
from any chance at wonder and love
and leaving your daughters
ruminating in the uncertainty
of being headstrong and full force,
holding the frail image of manhood
they were left to create.

And in that town by the sea,
your children exalted your absence
on fabricated stories of a glorious exit and eternal heartbreak.
Because the truth,
though simple and ordinary,
lacked rhyme and reason to justify the results.

Human is what I am for now

Who I am is an eternal search,
a driving force to pierce the atmosphere,
a strive to not simply occupy space,
but to live, to slither in the bliss of existence.

The search is independent,
a detached walk with loneliness,
a complicit understanding with solitude,
a daily negotiation with the eternal outcome.

A 26-inch gap
between brain and heart,
hollow space I breathe into,
and the simple connection to life
reestablished by the prompt to exhale.

May I remain gracious and aware
throughout this practice of being,
that tears flow, as feelings do.
As emotions transform,
so does the expression of demise.

A reminder,
that I'm not stagnant or eternal,
that nothing of this experience is permanent,
that everything is in motion at all times, as am I.

Fleeting

She marveled
at the possibility
of greatness, but
the very thought
was exhausting,
going against the tendency
of inherited traits
and the burden of grief,
weighs heavy on the ankles.
Instead,
she gathered
moments of joy,
pleasant moments
of intensity,
moments of truth
that gave wings to fleeting steps
over once-layered bricks.
Honest, transparent,
breathable moments
held in the safety of her body,
felt in invisible ripples of energy,
rhythmic pulses on her hands.
When she smiled,
mostly against her will,
fighting back human nature,
giving way to simple joy.
In those instances,
she was magic.

Feeding love

I get genuinely sad when I finish my food,
to think the last bite as inevitable,
an early onset nostalgia,
detected as each swallow concludes
with a soft, reminiscent sigh.

An intense moment lived in the here and now.

Slow
          chews.
                    Deep
                              breaths.
Preliminary
yet subtle actions to imploding flavor
over bursting salivary glands.

A mouthwatering,
eyes closed,
sensual,
and unique,
experience,
depicted only in memories
of over-generous pleasures
and the stillness in the aftermath,
leaving tiny souvenirs
scattered on the corners of my mouth
longing
          for
                    that
                              last
                                        bite.

Like the trees

Be like the trees,
severe and stoic from a distance.

Voluptuous, serene, and grand
upon a closer encounter.

Each protruding branch
a commemoration to life
and the opportunity for rebirth.

In each crevice and nick,
imprinted the stories
of all that have come for solace and
shade.

Be like the trees,
the seed it once was
contained in wet soil and darkness,
hidden complicity with the Earth and
its embrace.

Burst at the seams, drop roots on
instinct,
an unbiased harmony with nature,
release and transformation are
intended outcomes each season.

Be like the trees,
magnificent destiny already contained
within.
A tree isn't working on their dream,
they are the dream,
even below the ground,
in the darkness of layered earth,
seeds sprout roots fierce
enough to pierce conditions
in search of light and ingenious ways
to endure.

Discreet and strategic
whose age is not hidden or tragic
and only apparent in fine, wide,
and evenly-spaced lines as evidence of
significant growth.

A tree grows new wood around its
scars,
though they stay forever within.
Proving memories evolve and
transform
in the generations of those who come
barefoot to redeem their truths.

In a world where we are almost nothing, I built a purpose

It is not humanly possible to stay
happy,
    we don't stay anything.
What an injustice to the grandiosity of
our being
    to rob ourselves of feeling anything
other than happiness
    because it is not allowed,
    appealing,
harmonious, or eloquent.
It is, however,
    toxic and overly sensitive
because to feel
    is to appear human.
A typical idiosyncrasy -
    as it usually has nothing to do with
you and everything to do with the
discomfort it gives everyone else.

They don't know what to do with you
when your nostrils flare,
spit ejects from your mouth,
tears drop and your forehead wrinkles.
The transformation is a reminder of
their own deficiencies.

It is disturbing to think we are subject
to feeling happy
because we should not feel anything
but.
I want to feel it all.
Anger and its metallic residue on my
tongue
Frustration gripping at my throat,
shattering the sound of my voice,
provoking tears that burn like paper
cuts.
Happiness is not a state of permanence
or a specific location.
Rather, it is a process,
an ETA that depends on a very
personal journey,
    an arrival,
    a road walked many times before,
    of reminiscent flavors, sounds,
    and sensations.
It is a sense of heightened awareness,
    gratitude,
    wonder,
    plenitude.
Where you need nothing else but to
bask in that moment.

The time will come

Constant distraction from a list of possibilities
        can result in effective procrastination.

Dwindling hours under such pressure,
        succumb into minutes fading,
        into seconds tick-tocking to the countdown of the inevitable.

Time allotted for today's mission of breathing
        and being a *whole heart* or partially fragmented human–
        Either way, it is 24 hours.

Providing amplitude to sit with what is,
to contemplate infinity and its possibilities.

Time to feel my eyes open inward
        and watch the wonders of life inverted.

Simultaneous - coexistence and ultimate survival
        contained in the stillness of my body
        visible and palpable only through the bursting void
        and uncomfortable safety in waiting for it to pass.

This moment, lacking in hope,
        in spite of an abundant memory,
        leaving the lost in the graveyard of experience.

This fire in me had to be dealt with

Behind still, wide eyes,
lay a raging spirit
conditioned to behave,
to swallow
any revealing evidence
of imperfection,
rounded curves invisible,
only mentioned in their absence
impure passions tamed between distorted mandates.

Inside
a mouth left agape,
an emerging voice
lodged between desire and the airway
where it never quite disappeared,
though I always wondered where it went,
when I most needed it.

I developed a keen sense of observation
as life happened outside of myself,
and the fire burned within.
After sharp turns, and
going hard to landing soft.
The fire dimmed to ashes
where the worst moments
became a crucial part
of redemption.

That insatiable child
who knew there was more
and wanted it all
learned, by default,
to live with what she got.

The toxic luxury of being

I've spent a lifetime
trying to figure that out.
Answers have come in
varied forms.
Some liquid,
some gas,
some solid
In the taste of imported
beers,
cigarettes, and women,
and a few slip-ups with
opposite sex.
Unintentional, of course.
Or were they?
Nevertheless, all
ephemeral.
The answers have come
from the search inside.
For that little light
that never completely
dimmed.

I've come to find that
five minutes of now is
worth a whole lifetime
of before.
Before I could hear my
voice,
before I could hear my
heartbeat,
before I could taste my
tears,
before I could look up
from the mirror, and
stare into those eyes,
to find eternity.
Five minutes of that,
over and over would be
enough

So, I would never
recommend, suggest, or
imply
that you should know
yourself before anything
else

because I have come to
find out
that things don't
happen in any
particular order
with expected outcomes
already calculated.
I learned that to know
myself I had to go in
deep.
I had to be quiet.
be still, while terrified,
fearful of leaving this
existence without those
five minutes.

Every day, every hour,
sometimes every five
minutes, I go through
this,
and I become a little
less scared of being, a
little more of me shows
up.
A little less afraid to be,
and a lot more willing to
enjoy it.

Sad becomes me

There's an eternal chokehold
allowing minimal gasps
of short and shallow breaths.
A slow and steady postnasal
drip

drop

drip.

Accumulated peach pits at the back of
my throat, make it hard to swallow yet
another devastation.

Ripples sync to the beat of a heart
that pumps much faster in response
to the news; that isn't new at all,
but a daily addition to the list of
tragedies;
an odd amount of lesser humans as a
result.

I've grown unethically comfortable
with the monotony.

As if life just happens
or stops, turns off, ceases or not.

Waves of nauseating sadness at the
scent of death, emerged from the
mixture of stimulus and response
moving to and through every nerve in
my body,
leaving traces of stillness
after the residual turbulence settles in.

Eyes that tingle and pores that expand
wide enough to exude a tear,
one at first though quickly many.
Drip.

Drop.

Drip.

Ripples synced to the beat of a heart
that pumps much faster in response
to the news that isn't new at all.

Señora

Whenever someone calls me *Señora*,
I instantly think - your mother!

I look around to find the culprit
and gasp loud enough to display my
obvious indignation.

Not that I find it offensive.
But *¿Señora?* Me?
Señora is my mom, or yours, or
anyone else's mom!

But I guess it's beginning to show.
Perhaps it's the lack of care and freer
thoughts that come with achy bones
and unexplained insomnia.

Maybe it's the lines that encase a wider
smile or the cackle in various pitches
that escape in sync with the power
of a belly laugh - creating a rhythmic
percussion,
accompanying a most delightful
conversation.

Perhaps it's in my eyes, in their shades
of brown and gold, adding foliage
to the appearing roots in the skin
around them.
¿Señora?
Me who feels ageless, evolved and
transformed and had birthdays
that I didn't think would come. I've
celebrated the temporality of losing
myself in a dance, in the ocean, in a
woman, and on her.

Señora with that old soul,
and divine obsession with bags of all
sorts, to hold memories as evidence.

I've arrived in grace and no major
damage.
My best self, a bit out of breath but
with very little gray, at my best weight,
regardless of the numbers on the
scale, which I now choose to step
on, to measure illusion rather than
density.

Perhaps the departure took 30 years,
and an extra five to allow for
adjustment,
because long before the state of
Señora, there was a time when the
future was futile.
Now that I'm here, I'm sure it's not a
destination, but rather a daily
succession.

Heart search

My heart left my body long before I could double knot my shoes.

Making a subtle enough exit to leave no trace,

evidence or illicit memory to fabricate its departure.

Slithered under the door frame, absorbed onto wet concrete.

Nine years.

The last time I checked on my heart,

it had been nine years, 78 thousand 840 hours,

three thousand 287 point two-five days,

Only then was the lapse in time an obvious acknowledgment.

by then, I'd forgotten the rhythm of it's beat,

a dream once so desired, now sounded like faint ripples

slipping through my fingers and now relaxed hands

in simultaneous drips echoing on the laminate floor.

It is in this stillness that I am swallowed

by the silent memory of who I was then

because it is also in this silence, and only in it,

that I found bravery to live.

Child and beasts

Nightmares.
Sometimes monsters turn into beasts
that
claw with no mercy at her most
vulnerable memories.

A blunt beak, picked ravenously at her
deficiencies,
scaly lips sucked at her lacks,
a high-pitched shriek, taunted her
absences,
tearing each one from memory.

Creating permanent strain on her
heart,
thrusting life out of it in every pump
with massive, gentle, gripping hands.

Almost loving.

She sat there taking it all. Not
recalling if it was ever different before.
Anguished and empty,
dismissing any memory of joy.

Feeling the moisture of darkness on
the walls, soaking through her soul.
Dripping in continuous beads down
the trail of her spine.

No one would be able to tell her
what should have been.

Subdued but not frozen,
until she was able to transform.

Not the beasts into angels
or the memories into joy,
but herself and her perspective.

Eyes unfathomed,
Wilder, relentless and with a softer
heart.

The same beasts licked her wounds,
with such meticulous care;
crucial components in rebirth from
ashes to joy.

She has soaked their fur with her tears,
She learned to look back,
trusting in their presence
pleading forgiveness for the sins of a
child
which bore no consequence.

Those ferocious beasts, carried her,
and it was in their arms that she felt
replenished and able to emerge.

Enough

I am not fully gay,
as if it required a uniform or secret
handshake, as if the right to pleasure
and exploration had to be embroidered
on the top right hand corner of my
heart,
exposed and at view for consideration.

I am also not fully female.
I do not check any of the boxes on the
list of established criteria.
Ambivalent enough to leave you
questioning.
The length I lack in legs, smile, and
temperament
I make up for it with an overabundance
of ass, breasts, and sarcasm.
Traits meticulously trained
under the regime of a disappointed
matriarchy, who always knew and
expected,
that I could and should do better.

I am a blunt and intrinsic force.
Step outside of yourself,
look at me from a different angle,
widen your perspective.
just enough for the thought of me
to remain embedded in your brain
waves,
to divert the course of a certain
molecular structure, forcing you to
peer into the abyss that is your ego.
Rearrange previously established
thoughts,
the very ones that make you judge
and condemn me for not being
enough.

Ask again. Let's converse about how
difficult it is to figure ourselves out;
of the sediments deposited on our skin
that has bloomed our humanity.
Let's dare for greatness!
Let me hold your hand through this
transformation so the virtue of
becoming enough pulses between our
palms
and we're reminded of why we keep
being born.

I am everything I've been

a lot less of who I was

and nothing at all.

I am everything I have experienced

only to realize that wasn't all of me.

A perfect ending to

gracious uncertainty,

an eternal red carpet for the woman

I've chiseled from uncured stone:

striving for awareness,

a little less needy,

more gracious and willing

to embody this body,

to ride its curves,

downhill, without harness,

headfirst and fully alive.

In flight

I watch people walk urgently past the aisle on the plane

on their way to the restroom.

A mischievous smile at the thought of a long wait

if I was in there making love to you.

Gentle kisses take time to fully register

at 36,000 feet in the air.

They're given on the lips to begin with,

then collapse down the hollow of your neck,

in sync with the turbulence and mid-air bumps.

Gravity may take over the intent of seduction,

given the compressed space that fits your body

interlocked around mine,

with only your grip keeping me upright.

Love takes a form unknown:

spread eagle over clouds and a nearing horizon.

Variety

There are kisses given and kisses received.

Kisses reciprocated,
lost between our lips.

Our roles as the recipients,
completely undefined.

There are long kisses,
short, eternal kisses,
fluttering along my lips as proof of love
and insatiable desire.

There are kisses that make me come
out of my body and felt in my soul,
that have rescued parts once deemed unkissable,
nourishing my existence.

There are kisses I hold within
as reminders of your absence
and kisses that accentuate it even more.

There are kisses on empty pages,
written and accumulated
through a collection of the senses,
with the privilege of being taken for granted.

Kisses competent enough to withstand
what we're conditioned to endure alone.

Dream keeper

Blessed be the pillow
that holds your dreams every night,
left with traces of galaxies traveled,
of jungles green,
of footsteps left on remote beachfronts.

On it left conversations
with notable beings
and answers to questions
you'd long ago given up on.

Perhaps upon awakening
you've no remembrance
of these nocturnal voyages
left embodied on her rectangular
feather-filled form
to pick up where you left off,
finish what you started
or begin all over again
upon your return.

An infinite amount of
recurring possibilities
take supernatural form
inside closed lids
bringing to life the unknown.

She keeps your dreams secret,
even from you.

In theory

It is the elements in heat
that beautify the female.
Accentuating the natural
flow of instinct and desire,
exclaimed in rhythmic moans,
adding a memorable soundtrack
to the developing scene.
A permitted embrace,
laid out for pleasure,
willing thighs sprawled in open disposition.
Between her legs,
a flutter of hummingbird wings
fluctuating inhibitions
and primal yearning,
boiling over internal tide pools
in unison with the pulse of the earth,
shaken to the beat of her heart,
fused and irradiated by the posterior silence,
sustaining strength,
gearing up for the next spontaneous combustion.

Conversations with my mother

We sit side-by-side
or face-to-face,
shifting positions
in an effort to achieve
an unpleasant level of comfort.
We've learned to be
with each other,
to embrace a once
dreadful silence
that claimed our sanity,
pointing fingers at
generational faults
unknown
and irrelevant
to our current existence,
a gaze that struggles
to maintain eye level,
challenging any trace
of pre-existing conditions
out of a love
most pure and confidential.
This secret language,
developed from need
and visceral love
each at war with our own
private battles,
daring to change
what we were led to believe
was true.
A loyalty so fierce,
it brakes mold
and confirms
this multi-dimensional bond.
All this before the first word
is ever spoken.

Telepathy

I want to tell you my story
And not have to say a word.

I'd like to show you my soul.

I'd like you to know all about me,
that which matters,
and that much more.

Let me gaze into you,
and become less afraid
to know me
through you.

Let's not stop at the point where two souls become one;
or frolic too long in the powerful,
yet useless gift of reading your mind.

But rather explore the vastness;
far beyond the worlds we think we know.

Where we become each other.

And it's no longer some abstract phenomenon
to be loved so wholesome and to feel I deserve it.

Dying since the day I was born

I was born on the day of the dead.

Barely.

The occasion turned out to be quite cynical
and precisely appropriate,
though birth seemed dire and uncertain.

For 72 laboring hours, death lurked close.
Lodged between my mother's contracted hips
leaving imprinted bruises on my neck
that absorbed the expected first cry
once I was yanked from her body.

I'd like to think
that for those few eternal moments,
it was her primitive howl
that restarted my heart
and called me back from the deep.

A whole existence to prove true
the ability of life and death,
to coexist as a concurrent plan,
subjected to a decision on impulse,
that may have changed the outcome.

Of the deep

In the vast immensity of the ocean,
      in its depths and varied scopes
         of dark, transparent and light,
            I find my soul floating on the surface.

Every pore of my slithering skin
      camouflaged,
         by its textures of fine,
            grainy, smooth, wet sands.

In its fury rebellion and eerie calm,
      a disguise for the inevitable
         and expected pumps of my heart.

In the echo that remains
      after its crashing waves,
         I hear the whisper of my name.

I listen, and she hears my silence,
      its motion and sway,
         a soothing caress to my existence.

So infinite and small,
      yet minutely distributed in every molecule,
         in every drop of water that composes it.

Broken
      down
         and rebuilt
            in each wave
               that crashes
                  ashore.

Cyclical

It's all just a moment,
instants that start
to be over at the very moment
they've begun.
Moments faded
into the abyss
setting in motion their demise.

This moment is now over,
and we're onto the next
before the next word is written,
the previous line has reached
its expiration date.

Moments pass
become predictable
yet remain unexpected,
accumulated instants
keeping us present,
alert, and certain
that the end is near
before the other has begun.

Invocation

My heart!

Faithful companion
of obscure times.

In exchange for lucidity,
a silent, reliable rhythm.

Loyal, ever-present, and
uncompromised
until my return.

The nerve of me
to ignore you
in moments of dire need
when you've kept me alive.

For taking every punch
without filter,
I do apologize.
My heart!

Know that I do listen
in spite of myself.

I hear you in the silence,

I find you there,
where you've gotten heavy,
drowning in tears
I've chosen to swallow.

My heart!

I plead with you
to keep beating,
keep risking each step
taking me deeper
into your chambers.

Let me wear you on my sleeve,
pinned for safety
and ensured survival.

My heart!
for your presence,
devotion,
love and eternal rumble,
I'm in debt to you.

Too heavy to carry much longer

You just never know
what secrets lie
parallel
to a quivering smile
held wide through clenched teeth.
What it took
from within
to make an appearance
on the mask allotted
for the day's daily tasks.
What made bones rattle
in the darkness
of closet-enclosed shadows,
the very ones that dared
a dance with agony,
as if no one was watching
to the beat of his own demise.
An exhausting feat
that killed his spirit,
annihilating any trace
of the invisible digits
wrapped
around his throat,
sucking the life
from his soul
perhaps long before
he made the choice
to take it upon himself.

Tell it to the river

She, in all her wild nature,
carried your soul through quantum
leaps
and unexpected turbulence.

Kept you upright through a struggle
you previously and cautiously avoided
but silently proclaimed.

Tell her your secrets written in code,
embedded in the uniqueness of your
fingerprints.

It is only her that is able to decipher
the scrolls extracted from the gasps of
breath you were able to borrow.

You and her.
An intimate encounter.

A rebirth of sorts.
All resistance transformed to will
by its amniotic elixir.

Provocative thrusts expelling you
from its cushion and comfort
into an act of surrender,
to abyss of unknowns,
of instinct and revelations.

Your skin, permeable to its liquid balm
and its long-term benefits,
smoothed crevices,
nurtured and curated with her
indomitable strength.

You allowed life to birth you,
succumbed to its will;
now or never became an affirmative
always.

All ways.
Every day after and since.
A once matted and dormant fierceness,
embellished by the elements,
polished to a practical transparency,
suits you so well.

Eyes wider in disbelief, but body felt.
A witty strut in massive silence.
Dripping.

A fearless existence

The god that we fear
stares back from the mirror
every day, if we dare to see
that we are that which we fear.

It's not some external force
it's not circumstantial blame.

It is, however, generational curses
ripened and replanted in our veins.
What we fear to look at is ourselves
with equal parts despise and grace.

For we are also fully capable
of divinity and love
and gentleness and understanding
and perspective and maturity.

Created in an image that holds us to those truths
that we have forgotten over time and again.

What would jesus do and
thanks be to god,
would become personal phrases
directed accountability and the honor that those entail

Can we direct our faith back to humanity?
Back to each other?
Can we restore ourselves
in the eyes of the god that we fear
and fear ourselves enough to become it?

Redemption is a variant shade of bruised glory

The color purple runs alongside
the length of our arms,
interwoven through arteries,
spiraled through veins,
down the stretch of our backs,
around each vertebrae,
a system of collective communication,
protecting every bone
allowing us to bend like reeds in wetlands,
in ways unimaginable,
without breaking.

It's the precise hue embedded in our inner palette,
vibrant on our lips
as breath ceases to run through them;
on our fingertips when they've reached
an absence of warmth;
on skin cut open, layers exposed,
revealing in distinct tones,
the progressive healing that is occurring.

Digressing from heliotrope to amethyst,
blended into violets,
blooming into plums,
diluted into lilacs,
to reveal the mended dermis–
smooth and transformed from its original state.

The color purple is metamorphosis,
giving wings to the gashes and wounds,
redeeming our courage to live.

Meek and mild

Women exist or cease to,
with an explicit mandate,
quiet and silent
to not attract attention -
the less you notice, the better.

To not laugh out loud, with a wide
open mouth and disfigured face,
lips almost blue from lack of air,
from trying to talk through the
laughter.
Not like that, or in any other way.

Don't let your age show
nor the courage,
nor the belly,
nor the neckline,
much less the mustache
or the desire to fuck.

Enjoyment and pleasure, brutalized,
diminished to an exploited sex,
of fake and non-existent orgasms.

Believing that you defy time
and gravity.
Maintain neat, impeccable,
discreet and hidden,
with a lost gaze,
as if you weren't looking.

Don't you get angry,
don't scream,

It is better to be safe than sorry.
Having learned that being happy is
complicated
and compromising.
So it's scheduled
for another day,
when there is time
and if it's god's will.

So never.
Until it disappears.
It's better to settle for what's there.
That way you don't get noticed.

Thus, life loses its grace,
and you lose at life.

Poética

We are the paper thrown into the fire after being sworn to eternal secrecy.
Realities and undeniable facts succumb to flailing ashes that burn out inevitably,
but remain embedded in every spark;
gifts to bring warmth and comfort,
as we sip on chamomile and honey.

Our bodies avid receptors to its inspiration,
mesmerizing our fears in it's dance of power,
transforming mere yellows into gold,
And blues into ...
Well, the blues remain the blues.

To our darkness,
tenderness.
To our worries,
calm.

All auto-generated attributes found in the words of poets.

We are the poets,
we are the creases in the crumbles of the initial draft,
Thrown across the room, in an ambitious effort of three points into a can,
that more than trash holds evidence.
It lays in an increasing pile, around it and never in.
Anticipating our return to unfold and smooth out the creases.

because there is always something to be rescued -
a word or two,
a phrase or some,
as we create with the discarded,
a realm of possibilities.

Acknowledgments

The first time I heard Andy Sanchez at a La Palabra open mic in February of 2020, I was left profoundly moved. At my request, he graciously agreed to meet with me and informed me of the Community Literature Initiative (CLI). It was because of that encounter that I dared to dream.

Thank you to my classmates and instructors at CLI, for your feedback, for every opportunity to workshop alongside your talent, for keeping me inspired and accountable, and for the joy it was to share space with you.

Friends - all of you who had read my work and called it poetry long before I had any capability of acknowledging it. Your belief that I had something valuable to share with the world has kept my determination afloat in times of procrastination and self-sabotage.

Judy and Linda, I love us and our ever-evolving friendship. I am a better person for it. Thank you for taking the journey of a lifetime with me.

Mom, who looks at me in ways no one else ever will. All the good in you is good in me. Thank you for the wings.

Sister, who loves me and accepts me just the way I am. Thank you for your unconditionality. I am profoundly proud of the woman you are.

Brother, I honor every reason you have found to keep going.

Father, a man of few words and intense silence. Thank you.

The CLI book production team: Valentina Gomez, Enrique Martinez & Kim Gaeta, your suggestions, edits and ideas to enhance my work were all gracious and respectful. You must know that I've received so many compliments on the layout, cover design and color. I'm so grateful for your collaboration and ability to capture my idea!

Camari Carter Hawkins and Mama's Kitchen Press, for listening to my pitch at the Author Draft and for the opportunity to publish my book. I will forever be honored by your essential part in fulfilling my dream.

To my Biodanza community - for all the times our gazes crossed and I remembered who I am. It is a joy to dance alongside you.

This book was crafted in an effort to transform the parts of me that weren't working out—to be able to dance through them with love and grace, to transform them into dreams come true. I could not have left this life without completing it. It is because of this I can embrace myself as a poet.

About Deyanira Contreras

Deyanira Contreras is an emerging poet, childhood education teacher, and Biodanza facilitator; completed training and certification from the Los Angeles School of Biodanza, in Southern CA and currently co-facilitating a weekly group in Des Moines, Iowa.

A lover of life, coffee, words, the beach and the human spirit - in that order; or any other!

All things can be true /Todo puede ser cierto is her first publication.

Born in Ensenada, Baja California, Mexico, migrated to Southern California in 1984 and relocated to Des Moines, Iowa in April 2023, where she lives with her partner and their cat, Affogata.

Other Books by Mama's Kitchen Press

I'm Writing to Tell You by Jaha Zainabu

Sown in Light: poetry for the forgotten soul by Tekira Briscoe

Just Be Honest: a poetic invitation to liberation by Alexander James

Sorority of Bereaved Mothers: poems and stories from Black Women on pregnancy loss and infertility, Edited by Camari Carter Hawkins

Shooting Stars At Sky: the poetry of play, Edited by Mike Bonifer

Available at www.mamaskitchenpress.com

Otros libros de Mama's Kitchen Press

I'm Writing to Tell You by Jaha Zainabu

Sown in Light: poetry for the forgotten soul by Tekira Briscoe

Just Be Honest: a poetic invitation to liberation by Alexander James

Sorority of Bereaved Mothers: poems and stories from Black Women on pregnancy loss and infertility, Edited by Camari Carter Hawkins

Shooting Stars At Sky: the poetry of play, Edited by Mike Bonifer

Disponible en www.mamaskitchenpress.com

Acerca de Deyanira Contreras

Deyanira Contreras es poeta emergente, docente de educación infantil y facilitadora de Biodanza; Completó la capacitación y certificación de la Escuela de Biodanza de Los Ángeles, en el sur de California y actualmente co-facilita un grupo semanal en Des Moines, Iowa.

Amante de la vida, del café, de las palabras, de la playa y del espíritu humano -en ese orden- o cualquier otro!

Todo puede ser cierto /Todo puede ser cierto es su primera publicación.

Nacida en Ensenada, Baja California, México, emigró al sur de California en 1984 y se mudó a Des Moines, Iowa en abril de 2023, donde vive con su pareja y su gata, Affogata.

El equipo de producción de libros de CLI: Valentina Gómez, Enrique Martínez y Kim Gaeta, sus sugerencias, ediciones e ideas para mejorar mi trabajo fueron amables y respetuosas. He recibido muchos elogios por el diseño del libro, la portada y el color. ¡Estoy muy agradecida por su colaboración y capacidad de plasmar mi idea!

Camari Carter Hawkins y Mama's Kitchen Press, por escuchar mi poema en el Author Draft y por la oportunidad de publicar mi libro. Estare siempre honrada por su parte esencial en el cumplimiento de mi sueño.

Este libro fue elaborado en un esfuerzo por transformar las partes de mí que no estaban funcionando, para danzarlas con amor y gracia, para transformarlas en deseos cumplidos. No podría haber dejado esta vida sin completarla. Es por eso que puedo considerarme poeta.

Gratitudes

Agradezco la primera vez que escuché a Andres Sánchez en un micrófono abierto de La Palabra en febrero de 2020. Quedé profundamente conmovida y a petición mía, accedió amablemente a reunirse conmigo por Zoom para informarme sobre la Iniciativa de Literatura Comunitaria. Fue gracias a ese encuentro que me atreví a soñar.

A mis compañeros de clase e instructores de CLI, gracias por sus comentarios, por cada oportunidad de exponer mi trabajo a la par de su talento, por mantenerme inspirada, responsable, comprometida y por la alegría de compartir espacio con ustedes.

A todos ustedes que leyeron mi trabajo mucho antes de que yo tuviera la capacidad de reconocerlo. Su creer de que tenía algo valioso que compartir con el mundo, mantuvo mi determinación en tiempos de procrastinación y autosabotaje.

Judy y Linda, nos amo y nuestra amistad en constante evolución. Soy una mejor persona por eso. Gracias por emprender el viaje de mi vida conmigo.

A mi mamá, que me mira como nadie más lo hará. Todo lo bueno en ti es bueno en mí. Gracias por las alas.

A mi hermana, que me ama y me acepta tal como soy. Gracias por tu incondicionalidad, estoy profundamente orgullosa de la mujer que eres.

A mi hermano. Honro cada razón que has encontrado para seguir adelante.

A mi papá, un hombre de pocas palabras y de silencio intenso. Gracias.

A mi comunidad de Biodanza - por todas las veces que nuestras miradas se han cruzado y recuerdo quién soy. Es un placer danzar a su lado.

Igual y si

Las mujeres existimos,
o dejamos de,
con el mandato explícito,
callado y silencioso
de no llamar la atención -
entre menos te notes, mejor.

De no reír a boca abierta y carcajadas,
con el rostro desfigurado y labios
casi azules por falta de aire,
tratando de hablar
al mismo tiempo que reír
y llorar de la risa.
No rías así, ni de ninguna otra
manera.

Así la vida pierde su gracia,
y tú la vida.

Que no se te note
la edad,
ni el coraje,
ni la panza,
ni el escote,
mucho menos el bigote
o las ganas de coger.

Usted pulcra, impecable,
discreta y disimulada,
con la mirada perdida,
como que no te das cuenta,
de nada.

El disfrute y el placer brutalizado,
disminuido a un sexo explotado,
a orgasmos fingidos e inexistentes.
Creyendo que desafías el tiempo
y la gravedad.
Que no te encabronas,
ni gritas,
ni eres capaz de hacerlo, por miedo
a verte fea y menos mujer.
Que es mejor prevenir que lamentar.
Que ser feliz, resulta complicado
y comprometedor.
Así que queda agendado
para después,
para luego,
cuando haya tiempo
y si dios quiere.

O sea,
nunca - hasta desaparecer.
Será mejor conformarte con lo que hay.
Así no te haces notar.
Y la vida se va igual.

Descenso y despliegue

Habrá esos días
que la gravedad me absorba
al punto de quedarme
esparcida por la tierra.

Boquiabierta,
cara abajo,
ojos dilatados,
cada sentido
entrelazado
con las raíces existentes.

Fundida
en el fresco de su envoltura,
reconfortando
el agotamiento de mi alma.

Cada pedacito mío
estratégicamente,
colocado lejos de la cabeza,
permitiendo
que la sabiduría de los elementos
sea lo único
que intervenga en volverme a juntar.

Quedaré finamente decorada
con hilos de barro y lodo,
un adhesivo en cada herida
como huellas de conquista.

Apropiada
de un nuevo aprecio
por la piel que habitó,
por la necesidad
de sentir el aire que me acaricia.

Comprometo mi existencia
a dosis constantes de viento y sol,
de espacios abiertos
y al respiro consciente de la vida
misma.

Táctica y recuerdo

Hay momentos intensos
guardados en mi bolsillo,
envueltos en papel de china,
con olor a ti.
Hay frases importantes,
con el timbre de tu voz,
estratégicamente colocadas
en el crucigrama semanal.
Hay sonrisas mías,
secuestradas por encantos tuyos,
flotando en la superficie
de mi taza de café.
Hay placeres que vienen de manera natural,
tan sencillos como el respiro
he ingeniosos como el deslizar de tus manos
sobre mi silueta reflejada en la pared cuando no estás.
Y desde ya,
hay recuerdos tan únicos
grabados en cada molécula mía,
que únicamente se replicarán
el día que esta historia se repita.

Fase lunar

La luna se atrevió a acompañarnos esa noche
Era luna nueva
se estrenó con nosotras,
se dio a nuestro encuentro
Tan imponente y majestuosa,
plantada sobre el cielo oscuro
las estrellas rindiendo homenaje
al entorno vestido de gala para la ocasión
Mientras su única función era estar
- nada que hacer
Supo que estaría con la guardia baja
con la emoción a flor de piel
y el corazón a mil.
Y ella
se colocó lo más lejos posible
sin invadir el diminuto espacio entre las dos
Iluminando la posibilidad que surgía
Mantuve la mirada fija en ella
le pedía consulta antes de hablar o moverme
y en el ligero susurro del aire que soplaba, me decía:
Respira
Confía
Te escucho yo, ella y el todo
Ahí sentada, permeable, dispuesta y transparente
Me arrope de ella, de la luna y de mí.
Temblé de frío, de amor y de saber desde mi ser
Que la luna me sentía igual.
Me hizo guardia toda la noche
Aseguro mi desvelo
Me mantuvo alerta
Nada que hacer y tanto por sentir.

Lucha de poder

A cada momento,
toca apaciguar las bestias que me
consumen.
Detener su lucha constante
por apoderarse de mí.
Por tener la razón,
de no sé qué exactamente.

Tercas a su duelo y labor de
convencimiento,
ajenas, aferradas,
hambrientas y extremistas.
Paradas en puntos opuestos
anticipando la siguiente palabra,
pensamiento, acción -

Cualquier oportunidad es buena
para remover la consciencia
y convencerme que han creado un
monstruo.

A ver cuánto les dura el reinado.

Tranquilas, que hay momento para
todo.

Ni los impulsos me hacen mala.
ni logran espantar a nadie,
ni soy derroche de amor.
Hay que mantener cierta parte
intacta.

No gozo de tal transparencia,
pero si de un apetito insaciable
por descubrir el sentir de las bestias
que luchan en mi honor.

Habitar este cuerpo es
flujo constante de emoción,
asentarse en las sombras del sentir
y los extremos del todo o nada.

Así se siente estar viva en mí.
Bucear las profundidades sin
regulación.
Vivir hasta que duela todo.
Hasta que la piel se rompa
y el corazón se expanda,
hasta que los ojos se dilaten en agonía.

A lo que las bestias se aferran es la
lucha
que me mantiene viva.

Causalidad

Cómo fue que en ese justo momento levanté los ojos
Tu seguías indicaciones
Y yo buscaba una mirada
No es coincidencia,
si no cuestión de dirección -
y ausencia de límites,
Ahora incorporados a la conversación,
Previniendo alguna torpeza oral
Que comprometa un simple intercambio de instinto humano.
de cuerpo y emoción
que poquito quiere para ser captados.
Suposiciones mías quizás
Atentados contra mi vulnerabilidad
Con secuelas de placer
Esparcidas como hojas al viento
Por todo mi cuerpo.
Fue tu mirada la que encontré
Para darle tono a esta emoción
Que no importa la reciprocidad
Sino el hecho de recuperar
esta inquietud mundana, sagrada, resucitada
De encontrarme con la intensidad de mi placer.
Con el pulso vital de mi existencia.

Quiero decirte que te amo

No con en el contexto que encierra,
ni descalifica la amplitud de la palabra
Pero si con la intención pura
propia de la emoción.
Liberando cualquier necesidad de
tener que hacer algo al respecto
Comunicarte el gran descubrimiento
que comienzo a desenterrar en mi
Quiero decirte que te amo
Con todo lo que desata lo implícito de
la palabra
y el desafío de abordar la emoción
desde un punto de valor,
de empatía,
de honra
y pureza de intención.
Por todo lo divino que tuvo
movimiento en este encuentro.
Quiero decirte que te amo
Más no sé cómo lo tomes,
aunque me importa evitarte cualquier
incomodidad
Me es esencial en proceso y ejecución
llamar las cosas por su nombre
Con eso te digo,
que también estoy desarrollando la
sensibilidad que requiere hacerlo
Ser suave, gentil, madura, cuidadosa –
que me percibas de tal manera

y tomar lo que venga de ti con la
misma intención.
Quiero decirte que te amo.
Que navego en extremidades por
naturaleza propia,
que cuido mi propia fragilidad,
que soy voluble ante el amor
que lo añoro bajo mis propias
condiciones,
dudo de mi capacidad de recibirlo,
carezco por historia,
más me dispongo a él por mi propio
bienestar.
Que en este punto confío, que la vida
se ha encargado de mí, por más que le
pelee, me ha abrazado a pesar de mí.
Quiero decirte que te amo.
Me haces bien,
estoy dispuesta a tu compañía
a verme desde tus ojos,
a estar presente
y descubrir lo que traes para mí.
Te comparto mi ser,
desde el punto que lo vaya
descubriendo,
desde tu grandeza y la mía,
desde la comunión con el todo,
con la convicción que venimos y
vamos hacia el amor.
Quiero decirte que te amo.
Por qué no sé qué más se le puede
llamar a lo que es.

Revelaciones

Creía pensar que la vida me guardaba
algún secreto
De pequeña lo sabía por inercia,
que era el centro del universo.
Que era tan especial,
que en cualquier momento
me sentía totalmente feliz en este
ambiente.
Creía que la vida ponía a prueba
mi capacidad de observación,
de obediencia.
Así fui absorbiendo el entorno que me
rodeaba
y esa certeza se fue esfumando
Absorbí la miseria como herencia
familiar,
Todos en función de supervivencia.
Ellos guardaban el mismo secreto que
yo.
Fuimos cumpliendo el mismo
itinerario
Registrando marcas de
comportamiento adecuadas para
vivir,
Sin mucho que expresar en base al
secreto de la felicidad.
Embotellando rabias,
enfrascando insatisfacciones,

llenando la cajita de quejas y
sugerencias,
arrojadas a quien estuviera enfrente.
Ese fue mi primer registro de
supervivencia,
pelear, confrontar la vida y sus
atrevimientos en mi contra,
Con aires de indignación
y mi creciente complejo de
inferioridad.
Nos emparejamos en tamaño,
responsabilidad y rol
Llegué a abarcar más espacio
con emociones acumuladas
incesante furia de que yo no era de
aquí, ni de ellos.
Sin embargo,
siempre supe que pertenecía al todo;
era cuestión de recordar.
De acceder aquella inercia,
recordar la infinidad de donde vine
Bajar la voz,
suavizar mis movimientos,
para escuchar el murmullo del secreto
únicamente revelado ante tal libertad
De desprender el alma y abrazar mi ser.

¿Sentiste?

El despertar de un cuerpo adormecido
es un gran acontecimiento
Acto digno de celebración.
Es imposible ignorar tal intensidad
Me pregunto al regresar el alma al cuerpo
Al sentir como cada poro de mi piel
recuerda tu regreso
Al percibirte como parte del entorno
que minutos previos abandoné.
Merezco esta sensación de bienestar
¡Yo!,
creación viva,
funcional,
divina,
rara,
sensual
¡Yo!
a través de ti,
en resonancia contigo,
en fusión activa con todo.
Abro campo a la posibilidad de lo descubierto,
A integrarlo como referente de placer
Para saber qué se siente
sentir cada cosa por su nombre.

Tú en mí y viceversa

Hay respuestas de mi cuerpo acumuladas en la piel
Que me cubre los deseos insaciables de ti
Voy sintiendo como tu mirada despierta sensaciones
Alerta las caderas que comienzan por inercia su vaivén
en anticipación de lo que se aproxima,
Mis placeres empiezan su función.
Mucho antes de que llegue la señal al raciocinio,
Mi cuerpo encuentra tu último recuerdo almacenado
comienza el desarrollo de tu silueta sobre mi
La textura de tu piel cobra forma entre mis manos.
La gravedad de tu cuerpo en el mío.
Dentro, fuera, entrelazado,
ampliando suavemente los músculos contraídos
No estás, pero te encargas de mi
Me miras y atraviesas cada sentido
Me besas y te quiero mas
Me tocas y te guio a la reserva de agua contenida
No sé por dónde agarrarte
Donde comienzas o terminas.
Te quiero contra mí,
Dentro mío
Sin saber ni preguntar cómo o porqué
Nuestros cuerpos se encontraron
Quiero acceso a ti, entrar por las orífices de tu cuerpo
y salir mojada de ti
que solamente queden los residuos
del placer entre mis piernas
cómo lienzo de tu próxima aparición.

Idiosincrasia

¿Qué intercambio de palabras
podría resultar suficiente
para dejar de cuestionar
la intención de lo escrito?

Soy la que redacto en cada renglón,
y evolucionó en cada palabra,
ni la de ayer,
ni la de mañana.

En combinación con cada faceta,
cada emoción mía y eternamente cambiante.
En cada letra un amor eterno y particular,
propio de la misma intensidad que declaro
como testimonio de mi leve paso por aquí.

Escribir justo aquello
que me envuelve el corazón,
hace que me brinque el pulso
y retumbe mi ser.

Recordando
posibilidades e
interpretaciones
de lo que siento,
y deseo comunicar.

Lo cotidiano y lo perverso
enfatizado por pasiones latentes
que desprendo del alma
y plasmo en papel.

Incluso, por instantes,
logro separarme
dejar la consciencia,
la pregunta repetitiva
difuminando lo establecido
que nunca logré creer.

Siempre pensé que sería mejor madre

Aunque no siempre pensé en serlo,
resultó ser una falsa ilusión
previamente plantada en la psique femenina
basada en habilidades biológicas,
dejada al azar como sentencia y por añadidura.

El intento de producir una criatura con ciencia y amor,
disparó lo contraproducente en mi.

Realmente pensé que iba a ser mejor madre.
Resulte ser impaciente,
Hablo en voz alta, gritando incluso,
mi tacto es brusco, apresurado.
Soy impulsiva y torpe bajo la presión
de influir en un ser y dejar su humanidad intacta,
Únicamente después del impacto irreversible,
después que se me frunció el corazón,
logré descifrar lo que había en mi registro,
y aun así, creí que sería mejor.

Negros ojos magos,
desnudaron mi alma,
revelando insolencias.

No se mi amor,
si fuiste tú quien me dio alas
Pero créeme que el amor fue primordial
para saber que no era yo
quien te las iba dar a ti.
No así.

Lo único que tuve para ti
fue separar mi cuerpo, regresarte a la vida,
Feliz,
independiente de mí.
Eso es lo mejor que pude ser.

Pandemia

Este tiempo
de circunstancias
menos fáciles
resulta inevitable
distraernos de nuestra propia miseria.
¿Que hay en estas cuatro paredes
que nos haga vibrar,
que haga latir el corazón?
Busquemos el silencio para escucharlo.
Permitamos que nos retumbe la existencia.
En fin, estamos donde elegimos vivir
Mucho antes de la orden de encierro establecida.
La histeria,
en anonimato,
nos sucedía a diario.
Solo que era interna y más fácil de ignorar
Aun sabiendo que es el único camino.
Somos dignos de nuestra propia lucha

Resistencia

Me rehúso a pasarme la vida pidiendo respuestas baratas
en los momentos que exigen valor,
que me sacuden la existencia,

- para despertarme de mi misma
- para dar un paso afuera

y lograr recuperar lo que ya se:

- integrar las respuestas a mi jornada diaria
- dándole sentido al cambio,

sin pedir soluciones ajenas,
retomando la intensidad de mi ser,
y dando valor al descubrimiento.

Me rehúso a no vivir.

A mi divino ego

En tu presencia me siento
adorada y despreciada simultáneamente.
Qué intención tan específica y minuciosa,
de elevar y derrotarme a la par,
para ver si capte el mensaje
que pretendías darle de mi misma.

Que arrogancia la mía,
pensarte impenetrable.
Que lo mismo que piensas de mi,
Tiene obvias repercusiones en tu rostro.
Cada uno que hemos cruzado tu camino
una profunda grieta sobre tu piel.

Tu desinterés por aquellos que no alineamos bajo tu mando,
los que descaradamente nos atrevemos a cuestionar,
refleja tu propia lucha,
el coraje que te ha impulsado,
las barreras que has derrotado,
la actitud que has tenido que adoptar
para no engancharte en sensiblerías.

Proteges cautelosamente tu andar
manteniendo a distancia
cualquier muestra de necesidad
que pueda perjudicar la estabilidad que aparentas.

Te quiero tanto amada mía,
que desde un escalón bajo el tuyo
envió mi corazón,
deseo tu bienestar
y recibo el lento goteo de tus lágrimas.

De frente al amor

resulta que toda una vida sucede en 2 minutos
Ignoraba la fragilidad
del único momento presente.
2 minutos -
suficiente para salir corriendo,
bajar la mirada,
defender mi bestia,
amenazada por la brutal realidad.

Tiempo -
basta con levantar la mirada
lo suficiente para verme
en lo claro de tus ojos,
la transparencia de mi vida,
la abundancia de mi alma
a pesar de mí misma.

2 minutos de infinita posibilidad.
Jamás garantizados,
otorgados a favor de mí.

De frente al amor,
rodeada de la inmensidad,
de pie en espacio sagrado,
rendida al silencio de mi ser.

Cada caricia
una posibilidad ,
de expandir el placer
de restaurar su contenido en esos 2 minutos.

Con cada oportunidad crecí,
acompañé a mi tribu,
me enlacé a su alma
y ellos se dieron a mí.

Rindiendo homenaje a mi existencia.

Visceral

Emoción desinhibida
sobresale en luna llena.
Colocada en polos opuestos
entre el cielo
y la tierra,
entre pies
y cabeza,
entre vida
y la muerte,
entre tu
y yo.
La luna visible,
intensa,
y audaz,
llena
de luz
la oscuridad
y nos descubre transparentes
poniendo en evidencia
deseo,
instinto
y vanidad.

Vida y movimiento

Danzo para mi.

Para sentir y para dejar de hacerlo.

Danzo para mover mi cuerpo

y aquietar mi alma.

Danzo para mi.

Para recordarme y para olvidar.

Para pulsar con la tierra

y vibrar con el aire.

Para fluir con la vida.

Danzo para mirarme y conocerme,

por encima y más a fondo,

para abrirme los poros.

Siento la danza

en cada nota, cada verso.

como entra y sale de mí.

Danzo.

Hasta que me vuelva la vida.

Hasta que respire de nuevo.

Hasta que regrese a casa.

Hasta habitar-me.

Danzo.

Con intención.

Con ciencia y sin ella.

En cada encuentro,

una razón más para seguir danzando.

En tribu, en ronda,

con el todo y con la nada.

Que nunca es nada,

que soy yo.

Danzo.

Conmigo y por mi,

por mi vida

por ser contigo y por ti

Danzo.

Ser danzante

Cuando danzo,
escuchó la voz de una niña
sus sueños cobran ritmo,
sus palabras absorben melodia.
en sus ojos la infinidad

Mi cuerpo despierta
a las memorias que guardo desde entonces,
recipiente de mis mejores secretos,
obediente y leal.

Guiado por el sentir,
ha jurado protección,
rebosando sus propios límites;
volviéndose impenetrable.

Cuando danzo,
se tira al vacío permeable,
dispuesto,
añorando el próximo sentir.

Mi danza lo despierta.
Vibra ante tal liberación,
tiembla frente a la supuesta paz
que hasta hoy me ha protegido
Veo con las manos,
escuchó con la planta de mis pies,
toco con mis ojos
acaricio corazón,
percibo sus latidos y espero.

Paciente como nunca antes,
a que aparezca la sonrisa
mi compromiso con la vida.

Por fin me doy,
libre y dispuesta a la danza del placer.

Plegaria

Corazón mío.

Fiel compañero de momentos oscuros.
A falta de luz
intercambias silencio
sin comprometer tu lealtad,
hasta que yo decida volver a ti.

Corazón mío

Disculpa mi descaro al ignorar tu
presencia,
mi empeño de buscar fuera de ti,
lo que con cada latido me recuerdas
Independientemente de mí voluntad.

Corazón mío

Gracias por mantener mi vida,
por recibir cada emoción sin filtro.
Te escucho, te juro que si,
a pesar de cualquier ambivalencia,
ante la cual me rindo sin aparente
resistencia.

Corazón mío

No sé cómo hablarte para darme a
entender,
por eso te busco en el silencio,
donde yo te pueda escuchar,
donde te permita conmoverme.
Prometo dejarte la puerta abierta más
seguido

Corazón mío.

Te siento pesado en mi pecho.
creo que te estoy ahogando en
lágrimas.
Uno no puede andar por la vida,
destilando emociones al aire
Es por eso que a veces me las trago.
Pero tampoco se puede vivir
resistiendo los encantos

Corazón mío.

Sigue, latiendo,
sigue arriesgando cada paso,
sigue navegando profundo.
Hazme tuya con cada emoción.
Tienes en mi perfecto acomodo,
te llevo en mis manos y me consagro
a ti.
Prefiero sentirlo todo siempre,
por más intenso cual sea tu retumbe

Transparente estrategia

Quizás no debería decírtelo todo
Quizás debería guardarte algún secreto
Darme de a poco, con gotero
Pero es que me vas revelando hasta mis propios misterios
Me activas total disponibilidad a correr el riesgo sin razón alguna
Y se esfuma la intención de responderte en pausas
Que den espacio a interpretaciones.
Apareciste ante mi vulnerabilidad.
Ante la plenitud de mi alma.
Ante una mirada permeable y no te puede prevenir.
Ni siquiera traté de esquivar el flechazo.
Ahí me capté complacida,
mi deseo cumplido en forma de ti.
Ante tal magnitud; no hay deberías.
Así me doy a ti.
Llena de mí.
Porque supe que me recibirías de tal manera.
Lo que quieras saber de mí te lo diré.
No tengo secretos
Solo una historia que compartir.
Realidades que confesar.
Las mismas que me han puesto frente a ti.
Recibo la fuerza de cada paso, la intención del recorrido,
Y ahora frente a ti ya no estoy tan rota
Ni me delatan las heridas
Me entrego entera
A mi vida,
a sentirte en ella,
a disfrutar de tu placer
Al merecer tal emoción
Quizás eso es lo único que debería ser.
Por qué ya está siendo.

Reflejo

Gastamos tanto tiempo en discutir la jerarquía de un camino y otro,

Buscando diferencias,
argumentando ventajas,
tratando de convencer al otro.

Sin percatar las similitudes.

No necesariamente de la infinidad de caminos,
sino de la búsqueda que cada uno emprende en ellos.

Nos necesitamos presentes,
de la manera que nos sea posible –
y hay tantas maneras de manifestar presencia;
que siempre es posible.

Necesitamos amar la diversidad que nos marca,
conscientes que estamos hechos de la misma materia.

Aquello que nos lleva a escoger el camino,
cualquiera que sea,
no tiene razón precisa –
pero sí es diverso, complejo, ¡y compuesto de divinidad!

Conversaciones con mi madre

Sentadas
Lado a lado o de frente,
frecuentemente cambiando posición
física y de pensar.
Irradiando cierta impaciencia e incomodidad.

Por igual
hemos aprendido a estar juntas.
a abrazar
lo que una vez fueron
silencios incómodos
reclamos sin fundamento,
culpando a la vida
de una herencia inevitable
que ahora nos resulta irrelevante.

De repente se nos dificulta la mirada
frente al reto de vernos con amor.

Un lenguaje secreto,
desarrollado por necesidad,
cada una lidiando su propia batalla
Retando creencias de lo que debería ser.

Verdades escritas

Confío en la seguridad que me brinda cada letra.

Cada consonante y vocal conjugan sonido y pronunciación,
dando vida y sentido al formar las palabras.

Tomo inspiración de todo lo que me rodea,
en suspiros, sonrisas, lágrimas y sabores.

Encuentros propiciados por alquimia divina,
palabras dichas en voces conmovedoras.

Basta una sola para desatar infinidades.

Para ligarse a algún recuerdo silencioso.

Cómo lograr captar cada ilusión,
cada derrumbe,
cada amor que se prende y esfuma con intensidad.

Benditas palabras
con las que intento describir
las funciones básicas de mi existir y el tuyo.

Sabiendo que no es exclusivo
el latir del corazón,
la respiración agitada
o el volteo de pupilas.

Benditas palabras,
que me acarician el alma,
suavizan mis sentidos,
dando voz al brutal acto de vivir.

Huraña

Sé que tengo frágil el corazón,
que me fluctúa la soberbia,
que hay un eterno vacío en mi alma que no tiene nombre.

Frecuentemente cambia de significado,
que no encaja en el flujo común,
de vivir esperando que alguien te averigüe.

Hasta hace tiempo,
planeaba estratégicamente como eliminar tales atributos,
decepcionada y con los puños amoratados de esperar,
después de varios episodios de catarsis silenciosos
llegue a la conclusión que únicamente
me pulen la sonrisa, suavizan mis abrazos
y dan cierto toque de cinismo
justo y necesario
para mantener mi distancia
sin dar tanta explicación.

Frágil el corazón,
con pizca de soberbia
y un vacío innombrable

Me dan acceso a conversaciones transparentes e inspiraciones al azar.

Ilusiones

Eres esto, todo y aquello que un día pasado,
pero no muy lejano,
Escribí y decreté.

En esas temporadas donde hice uso de poderes intuitivos,
Casi casi de la magia...
negra quizás; dudo que blanca y pura,

Pues lo que pedía no era necesariamente sencillo.
En el momento precisamente inesperado,
Justo cuando la vida te sorprende dispuesta a hacer barbaridades
y te encuentra libre de culpas por las consecuencias,
En ese justo momento, me percaté acompañada.

Ni sutil, ni fugaz, ni desapercibida, si no, presente, imponente y sencilla,
De repente volteo y estas...aunque no sea así.
Más que nada te siento.

Lo más probable, es que no seas todo
Que todas esas barbaridades a las cuales estaba dispuesta entonces,
ahora las hacemos por dos.
Sería injusto privarme de tantas lecciones aprendidas,
para tener otra oportunidad de hacer lo mismo diferente.
Sería lamentable no caer de frente
por el solo hecho de saber que al extender la mano encontraré la tuya.

Lo inevitable de vivir

Se me fue la hora,
la fragilidad,
la consciencia del momento presente.
Eterno para unos.
Tedioso para otro.
Seguro para todos
Se me fue el minuto
en cuenta regresiva
desde el punto de entrada,
Se me va en cada respiro
Y ella tan propia y sutil,
Me permite los aires de grandeza
al sentirme competente,
Sabiendo de antemano,
que lleva las de ganar.

Oasis

Es en este espacio de tierra,
Con profundidades inmensas
Cuerpos de agua sumergibles
Cerros casi inalcanzables
Cielos infinitos
Y un sol que suele desvanecer al oeste,
Donde me encuentro pensando
En el momento que regrese
Será contigo...
Poder compartir estos sencillos placeres
Contigo.
Que en el simple gesto de voltear a verte,
Haga que mis sentidos vibren
Se profundice mi respiro y te absorba,
en el intento de permanecer en tu presencia
el mayor tiempo posible.
Que todo lo que nos rodea deje de ser reflejo
y se convierta en cuatro puntos cardinales
Que me rodeen el cuerpo
Para desvanecerme en ti.

Tu y mi placer

Si me expandieran las venas,
y fuera la piel transparente,
podrías verte deslizándo por ahí.

Tengo el cuerpo dibujado
con el roce de tus manos
y la emoción correspondiente
escurriendo entre las piernas.

Absorbo el calientito de tus labios en cada inhalación.
Mientras mis manos se deslizan en busca de tu ausencia.
Vibro solo de pensarte, siento el aire de cada exhalación sobre mi piel,
te miro, con la mera intención de fundirme en ti

Mi anatomía en plena función.
En ese espacio, rendida al deseo de saborear tu existencia,
de colgar sobre las curvas de tu cuerpo mi revivir.
La distancia marca las pautas,
afirma los pasos, regula la respiración.
Mientras registro lecciones de paciencia.

Me vienes en oleadas

Te vi por vez primera sentada de
espalda al mar.
Cómo es que ahora vienen los
recuerdos,
si en ese momento, fui directo a ti.

Hay un lapso de memoria física, pero
tengo la certeza
que te percibía en el entorno.

Particularmente el timbre de tu voz,
un ronroneo extranjero y seductor.

Caminas con impulso, cargando una
historia muy tuya,
dispuesta a aligerar el peso que te
pueda causar.

Habitas espacios medidos por los
kilómetros de viaje
que te traen a estas costas cada mes,
puntual y precisa.
Mantienes cierta ajenidad, al partir
con la misma disposición.

Eres todo un estuche de monerías,
de sonrisas y picardía inesperada.

Te acompañan aires de conquista,

que muy adecuadamente pretendes
distinguir.
Me expones a oleadas de deseo
adormecido,
Mides contacto, roce e intensidad –
propones amplitud de lo
anteriormente establecido,
hasta quedar perfectamente
acomodada en mi hombro.

Posición que te deja sujeta al pleno
sentir de mi corazón

Me retumbas la existencia.
Generas frecuentes destellos de placer.
Guardo el roce de tus manos entre la
mía como registro de lo sucedido.

Solo tú y la luna testigos entre esa
vastedad.
Nada fácil mantener la integridad
cuando predomina el deseo de
tomarte entre mis brazos,
probar a que sabe todo aquello que
viene de ti.

Te llevo dentro, en cada emoción,
cada espacio que abarco, cada
vibración.

Por qué tú me entraste por el alma.
Camino hasta hoy desconocido.

Equipaje genético

Vengo con la herencia de
mujeres fuertes,
macizas, robustas y
voluptuosas,

Cuyo cuerpo camina con
peso sobre la tierra,
cada paso impreso,
impulso preciso,
mirada fija en dirección
a su destino.

Vengo con la herencia de
hombres ausentes,
abrumados, constantes y
leales

De presencia
intimidante, escasos
de bullicio, llenos de
intención,

protectores y con el
corazón eterno.
Confirmo que nací
perfectamente equipada
con sabiduría ancestral,
semejanza física, y la
eterna búsqueda por
sanar una historia
repetitiva,
por revindicar nuestro
paso por esta vida.

La herencia pesa.
Desprenderme requiere
carácter, paso firme,
mente clara y un cuerpo
resistente, para
distinguir entre lo que
dejaré con ellos
y lo que, de ellos, venero
en mí.

Los encuentro en cada
mirada,
y sé que desde esa
infinidad ellos también
me ven a mí.
Invoco su presencia,
honro sus vidas,
celebro su camino y
disfruto el permiso
recibido para avanzar,
para mejorar la especie,
para pulir la misma
humanidad que nos une.

Lustrando mi alma,
danzando mi divinidad,
en un constante
reconocimiento del
espacio que fue forjado
especialmente para mí.

Yo hasta hoy

Aún me estoy encontrando acomodo.
Aún pregunto por mí.
Aún investigo qué más hay.

Resulta que tanto las preguntas como
las respuestas,
evolucionan,
son cambiantes y eternas.

Sigo sin saber nada,
aunque son menos los recuerdos,
en ausencia de imágenes
hay recompensa de emoción.

Ha sido cuestión de tiempo y
disposición,
llegar a este punto de mi vida,
con el corazón en la mano y la piel
expuesta.
De poder mirarme y honrar cada
paso, cada instinto.

De desarrollar la intuición -
Ese poder invisible que siempre supo
dónde llevarme

y este cuerpo que siempre siguió
indicación.
Me siento dentro.
Toda fisiología y función, en constante
actividad.
Con total disposición de encontrar
acomodo
y manera de ser en el mundo.

Se que a donde vaya, donde esté, y con
quien,
me vendrán noticias nuevas,
información a integrar
amor que sentir.

Se que soy,
que siento,
que pulso con el corazón
que he despertado desde la más
mínima célula,
que me toca recibir,
que merezco disfrutar,
experimentar mi cuerpo,
en armonía con todo lo que me rodea.

Sigo sin saber nada, pero consciente
de mí.

Invitada de honor

Tengo días con el oído de caracol
Con el llamado del mar
El retumbe de su eco
y susurro en espiral
Entrelazado entre su invitación
Y mi nostalgia de estar ahí
Hoy llegué y me recibió su inmensidad.
Con el rugir de sus mares de fondo y percusión
Impactando los soplos de aire
Que acariciaban mi rostro.
En cada paso que me acerca
Me seduce su espectáculo.
Disfruté la sinfonía en primera fila.

Sinfonía

Asumir elegancia,
cautela,
furia,
Intención
y tono,
Dejan al cuerpo satisfecho e
Inmóvil.
En recuperación breve
Repleto, pero siempre hambriento,
Danzando entre instinto y placer.
En cada encuentro
Entonando frecuencia,
ritmo y melodía
El rugir de los tambores
a la par del corazón,
El suspiro de la flauta
al son de un aliento
Crean un pulso simultáneo
Dónde se abandona el cuerpo,
descansa el pensar,
y somos
el placer.
En este cuerpo vivimos
irrumpiendo restricción
entonando incertidumbres
habitando la vida.

Alquimia de los elementos

Los elementos en celo,
embellecen a la hembra.

Ella permite su función,
En un flujo de instinto y deseo.

Abraza las ganas.
tendida al placer.
con los muslos dispuestos y
entre las piernas,
alas de colibrí.
revoloteando
entre inhibición
y libertad.
mientras hierve el agua
que desboca de su interior.

Vibra en fusión con la vida.

Al ritmo del placer.

El gusto y el silencio posterior,
regulan su respiro.

Los elementos en función plena,
sobre su piel humedecida,
recobran fuerzas para su próxima manifestación

Cíclico

Todo es un momento.
    Instantes
        que empiezan a terminar
          desde su inicio.

            Momentos que no duran.
              No es ese su propósito.

            Desvanecen en el abismo.
              Diluidos en la profundidad,
                desde su punto de comienzo.

            Por lo tanto este momento terminó,
              al instante de su comienzo.

          Al escribir la próxima palabra,
            el próximo renglón caduca.

        Y pasan los momentos
          de un instante a otro:
            constantes.

      Con la única seguridad
        de que empiezan su final,
          antes de comenzar el próximo.

Veladora de sueños

Dichosa la almohada
que arropa tus sueños cada noche,
Ella que es digna de tus penumbras,
en la que quedan rastros de tus recorridos
por lo verde de las selvas
o tus pisadas marcadas en la arena
de alguna playa recóndita.

En ella quedan encuentros con seres notables
que suelen dar respuestas a inquietudes,
que hace tiempo dejaste por la paz.

Quizás al despertar no recuerdes tus viajes nocturnos,
pero en ella quedan plasmados,
para retomarlos en tu próxima vigilia,
Dar cierre a los empezados,
o crear algo nuevo de lo que quedó inconcluso.

Una infinidad de posibilidades creadas durante el día
toman forma sobrenatural al volver a pegar los párpados.

Dichosa la almohada, que conoce de ti lo que a mí me es ajeno.

El Cuervo: maldición generacional

Partiste de este plano
mucho antes que yo entré en el.

Cuenta la leyenda
que te jugaste la vida a *full*,
en espera de alguna realidad,
que no fuera la evidente.
Rogándole al destino
que pagará siete veces el valor de la apuesta.
Un abanico sostenido en manos sudorosas,
tercia de ases y par de nueves
le dieron ventaja al oponente,
y a ti la vida te quedó inconclusa,
ahogada en un último suspiro.

Te sentí en los silencios de mi padre.
Silencios ausentes de cualquier asombro,
escasos de bullicio innecesario.
En la resignación y falta de entusiasmo
que hoy reconozco como herencia familiar.

Has de saber que así han partido varios,
con el corazón roto,
desolados.
De legado, una masculinidad ausente,
creada de fantasías
que superan el dolor de la realidad.

Aun, tu presencia permanece
un secreto enigmático,
denso y neblinoso
ahogando los secretos guardados
en la lealtad de los restantes.

Hembra

La divinidad femenina
se lleva en alguna parte del alma
Independiente de genitales,
biología o asignatura al nacer.
Su belleza es exquisita,
encantadora,
y de un deleite seductor.
Curvas que se hacen agua en la boca,
pestañas que escombran cualquier duda,
senos que nutren a la humanidad entera,
muslos que contienen nuestro instinto primal.

Como matriarca de mi propia existencia
rindo homenaje a este cuerpo
que me ha cargado en momentos
de indignación,
de vergüenzas acumuladas,
de pensamientos aniquilantes
atentos contra mi propia vida.
y la conquista de haber sobrevivido
las penumbras momentáneas
que en su momento parecían eternas.

Los secretos contenidos en este cuerpo
sobrepasaron sus límites
expandiendo sus pieles
en intento de caber en expectativas ajenas,
en un molde que nunca fue posible encajar.
Habitando la mortalidad de cualquier suposición,
me atrevo incierta, transparente
y dispuesta a vivir.

Resurrección

Le he hecho el amor a tres mujeres en esa cama.

Al comprarla
sabía que la quería fuerte,
maciza e inquebrantable.
De madera sólida
para sostener sueños,
contener descansos
o alentar insomnios temporales.

Nunca había pensado en eso
hasta hoy que considero deshacerme de ella.
Ella que en su momento fue grandiosa y
aparentemente perfecta,
hoy resulta bromosa y exagerada.

Tres etapas.

Tres vidas.

Tres mujeres.

Variedad de físico, cabellera y personalidad.

Ella sostuvo descubrimiento, frustración, ternura, placer
y ultimadamente
silencio.

Le he hecho el amor a tres mujeres en esa cama.

Tres caminos recorridos
y queda una sola huella en el colchón
a la derecha de la cabecera.

Tres mujeres se han tendido en ella
y una sola ha resucitado.

Catalizadora

*def.: Que atrae, conforma y agrupa
fuerzas, opiniones, sentimientos.
Que estimula el desarrollo de un
proceso.*

Lo tomo tan en serio,
responsable de que mi función
biológica, anatómica y existencial
No sean en vano.

Catalizadora.

Busco espacio en la tierra
que me fortalezca lo suficiente
decorando el próximo encuentro.
Con nuevos recursos,
sagrada ofrenda a mi
mejor versión.

Catalizadora.

Atraigo experiencia,
añoro su elemento de sorpresa, que
diluye cualquier resistencia.
Conformo,
clasifico por color y categoría,
alfabetizo
pretendo poner orden al caos
que disimula la vivencia más intensa.

Dibujo en mi cuerpo el simbolismo
del amor
y la pasión que he disfrutado.

Una excéntrica colección,
pedacitos de memorias,
fragmentos añejos,
amuletos de batalla colgados a mi
cuello,
repelentes de miseria.

Catalizadora.

De opiniones, experiencias,
sentimientos que me mantengan lo
suficientemente descompuesta
y eternamente consciente de mi.
Que sucedan emociones simultáneas,
paralelas
a la danza que emite mi cuerpo
Como su más vital función.

Ella desde mis ojos

—para J.G.

Camina anticipando la
próxima explosión,
el cuerpo en alerta,
vigilante y ausente de
cualquier comodidad.

La cabeza le trabaja a
mil por hora, tomando
minuciosos cuidados
para que sus pasos no
perturben el campo de
guerra.

Sus ojos siempre
abiertos, con la
particular habilidad
de detectar la única
flor que ha salido del
escombro.

Le corren las lágrimas
ante tal belleza.

Cuestiona cómo es
posible que la vida le
regalé estos pequeños
milagros.

Sus pensamientos
son perturbados con
preguntas
     cíclicas
     espirales
     y continuas,
cuyas respuestas
únicamente vienen con
el tiempo.

Está en constante
movimiento,
se le dificulta la quietud,
se atreve, pero ya no
corre,
ya no pretende escapar.

Se para de frente sus
demonios,
les da un beso en la
nariz y caen indefensos
ante tanto amor.

Ella es amor,
puro, noble y sincero,
de la mejor calidad.

Rasgos que ella logra
únicamente percibir
en el entorno, aunque
este mismo se esté
derrumbando.

Acostumbrada a las
batallas minuciosas que
la vida le ofrece,
arriesga la constante
tentación de
desaparecer entre la
multitud,
de evaporarse en una
última inhalación,
de perseguir una última
altura,
Y seguir contemplando
la vida desde otro plano.

Ella camina con capa y
escudo,
protege por instinto,
pelea por impulso,
sea necesario o no -
para ella siempre es
indispensable.

El latido de su alma le
recuerda que es
mundana,
que es transparente y le
indigna tal atrevimiento.

Cuando está triste,
saboreo sus lágrimas,
percibo su agonía.

Cuando está feliz, la
escucho sonreír, me
ilumina su alegría.

Lo es todo.

Solo falta que ella lo
sienta.

Paseo Existencial

En cada paso dado fuera de mí,
está marcado el camino de regreso.

Migajas esparcidas,
señalando pasos con la intención de volver.
Pedacitos de mí regados por vientos lejanos,
han germinado y dado frutos emotivos,
de euforia aguda y silencios añorados.

Regreso a mí.

A ese espacio imperceptible al caminar,
antes de que el talón toca el suelo,
donde el impulso del siguiente paso
es el que me devuelve el aliento.

Donde me encuentre,
tengo la certeza de que es por ahí.
Caminando, con paso firme,
pies cansados, piernas resistentes,
aclimatada a cualquier adversidad.

Inhalando el camino,
en respiros pausados, fluidos y calientitos.
Absorbo sus profundidades.
Cada llegada es a casa.

Donde quiera que sea,
llegó por instinto,
por impulso,
conquistando el camino
contribuyendo a un destino mejor.

TODO PUEDE SER CIERTO

Prefacio

Todo Puede Ser Cierto es una colección de lo que he llegado a comprender a lo largo de mi vida hasta este momento.

Es una combinación de ingenio, sarcasmo, deseo, valentía y placer. Una danza con la vida para comprenderme a mí misma y mi lugar en el mundo.

Me he dado cuenta de que estoy, como todos nosotros, en constante evolución y transformación: que somos más parecidos que diferentes.

Quiero que mis escritos reflejen eso: la vulnerabilidad que poseemos como seres humanos, en un esfuerzo por ser más amables, más suaves y más empáticos unos con otros.

Todos simplemente estamos aprendiendo a vivir, a hacer lo mejor que podamos, y lo entendamos o no, ¡no saldremos con vida!

Que nuestros encuentros sean abundantes, nuestra danza sea eterna y que cada día hagamos realidad nuestros propios sueños.

Índice

Esto está dedicado a ti, quizás no nos hayamos conocido y nunca lo haremos. Aun así, deseo que te veas con gracia y compasión, que te sientas un poco más humano, al leer estas verdades, que son sólo mías tal como las he descubierto. Pensamientos que me han salvado de mí misma en ocasiones. Palabras que vivo para incorporar en mi dia a dia y en una forma de ser en el mundo.

Toma de ellas lo que necesites.
Gracias por encontrar esto o permitir que te encuentre a ti.

All Things Can Be True / Todo Puede Ser Cierto
© 2025 Deyanira Contreras
ISBN: 979-8-9893829-9-6

Published by Mama's Kitchen Press
Austin, TX / Los Angeles, CA
www.mamaskitchenpress.com

First Trade Paperback Original Edition, 2025

Manufactured in the United States of America

Cover Art & Design by Kimberly Gaeta Brown
Layout Design by Emily Anne Evans

TODO PUEDE SER CIERTO

Deyanira Contreras

TODO PUEDE SER CIERTO

Alabanza por *Todo Puede Ser Cierto*

Con una visión personal y creencias universales bellamente estructuradas, Deyanira ilustra las complejidades del autodescubrimiento, la resiliencia y la identidad cultural. Una colección de poesía honesta y sorprendente que fomenta una comprensión más compasiva y empática de nosotros mismos y de los demás.

—Crystal Reyes, autora de *Wildflower Blooming*

Todo Puede Ser Cierto es una invitación tierna y a la vez valiente a desenredar nuestro sentido del yo en los mundos en los que vivimos. La colección debut de Contreras no es nada menos que la seguridad de una mano que nos sostiene, una compañera de palabras tejidas con intencionalidad y una mezcla de poesía elaborada para acompañarte a casa. Todavía no he encontrado una colección que sea más un espejo que *Todo Puede Ser Cierto*. Este edredón de poemas llama a la acción mi propio reflejo pidiéndole que se libere. En estas páginas de liberación, hay un anhelo, un consuelo y un hallazgo de autoaceptación, una exhibición liberadora de nuestros tabúes y un abrazo acogedor de los caleidoscopios que se encuentran en nuestras identidades. Contreras es un autor-arquitecto-artista de una hoja de ruta universal que llevamos con nosotros, mientras pintamos el lienzo de nuestras verdades, con valentía, abiertamente y con total audacia.

—RAVINA, autora de *Yellow*

A través de su mirada interna, Contreras nos invita a un mundo de profunda conexión humana y vulnerabilidad cruda, revelando la belleza y el coraje de compartir nuestro yo más íntimo.

—Andrés Sánchez, autor de *This Body*